1

NEW Cornerstone

PICTURE CARDS

ISBN-13: 978-0-13-524472-2
ISBN-10: 0-13-524472-2
EAN
9 780135 244722 90000

Pearson

Contents

New Cornerstone 1
Picture Cards

Pearson, 221 River Street, Hoboken, NJ 07030

Illustration and photo credits: 003 Paula French/Shutterstock; 005 Espies/Shutterstock; 007 K-Kwan Kwanchai/Shutterstock; 009 PCHT/Shutterstock; 015 Steven Russell Smith Photos/Shutterstock; 017 Guido Fuà/AGF Srl/Alamy Stock Photo; 019 XiXinXing/Shutterstock; 021 Serena Hsu/Zuma Press/Newscom; 023 Stocky images/123RF; 025 Rawpixel.com/Shutterstock; 027 Fotografiche/Shutterstock; 029 Maxim Cherednichenko/Shutterstock; 031 Christian Goupi/Age Fotostock/Alamy Stock Photo; 033 123RF; 035 Espies/Shutterstock; 037 Blend Images/Shutterstock; 039 Mihai Andritoiu/Alamy Stock Photo; 041 Goinyk/123RF; 043 Patpitchaya/Shutterstock; 045 F. Rauschenbach/F1online digitale Bildagentur GmbH/Alamy Stock Photo; 047 Brgfx/Shutterstock; 049 Svitlana Bezuhlova/Shutterstock; 051 Igor Gorelchenkov/Shutterstock; 053 Yan Lev/Shutterstock; 055 Martin Maritz/Shutterstock; 057 Andrey_Popov/Shutterstock; 061 PjrTravel/Alamy Stock Photo; 063 (T) I'm Guitar/Shutterstock; 063 (B) Daizuoxin/123RF; 065 Stephen Coburn/Shutterstock; 067 Puay Ng/EyeEm/Getty Images; 071 Tinna2727/123RF; 073 Wavebreakmediamicro/123RF; 075 Lentilka/Shutterstock; 077 Cristi180884/Shutterstock; 081 Kristi Dodo/Shutterstock; 085 Katatonia82/Shutterstock; 087 Evastudio/Shutterstock; 089 Koldunov/Shutterstock; 091 Lane Oatey/Getty Images; 093 Sailorr/Shutterstock

ISBN-13: 978-0-13-524472-2
ISBN-10: 0-13-524472-2

animal

animal

backpack

backpack

ball

ball

birds

birds

blossom

blossom

bought

bought

butterfly

butterfly

carnival

carnival

celebration

celebration

cello

cello

chef

chef

community

community

costume

costume

country

country

crew

crew

cruise

cruise

delicious

delicious

doctor

doctor

dragon

dragon

duckling

duckling

envelopes

envelopes

feathers

feathers

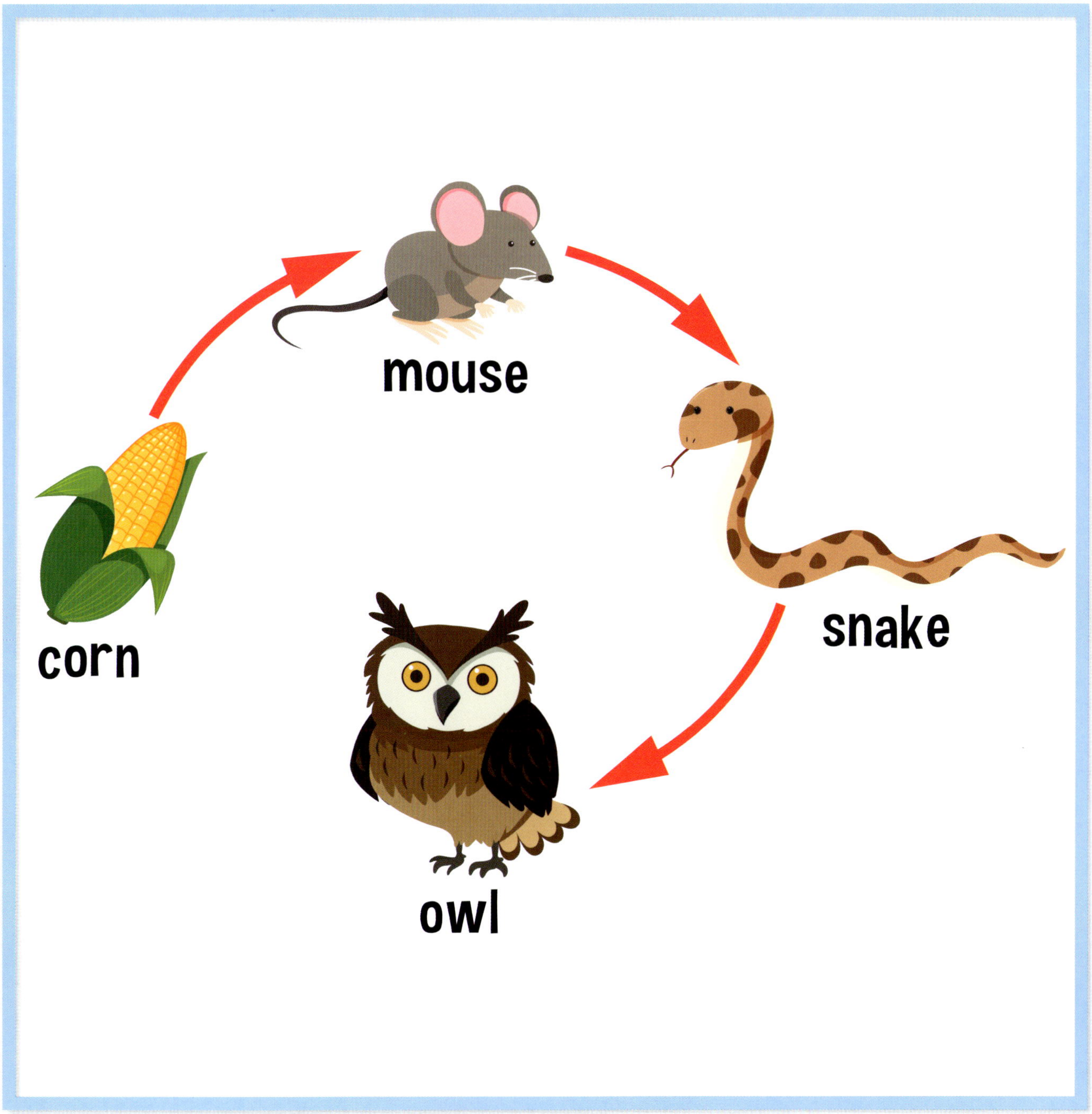

food chain

food chain

friends

friends

frog

frog

fun

fun

hippopotamus

hippopotamus

letter

letter

music

music

neighborhood

neighborhood

new

new

package

package

parade

parade

people

people

play

play

project

project

pumpkin

pumpkin

snack

snack

soccer

soccer

symbol

symbol

3

three

three

tortoise

tortoise

waddle

waddle

water

water

welcome

welcome

world

world